Everybody Hides

*How the Pandemic Unmasked
Who We Really Are*

by
BRIAN TURNER

Copyright © 2025 Brian Turner

All rights reserved.
No part of this publication may be reproduced, distributed, or transmitted in any form or by any means, including photocopying, recording, or other electronic or mechanical methods, without the prior written permission of the author, except in the case of brief quotations used in reviews, articles, or scholarly analysis.

This is a work of creative nonfiction. Some names, locations, and identifying details have been changed or fictionalized for the sake of storytelling. Any resemblance to actual persons, living or dead, is purely coincidental.

For permissions, inquiries, or bulk orders, please contact:
 hi@heybbt.com
 www.heybbt.com

First Edition
ISBN: 979-8-9931382-5-1

Printed in the United States of America

Table of Contents

What Was..4
Author's Note... 6
Chapter 1: Behind Closed Doors..........................8
Chapter 2: The Masks We Wore........................ 13
Chapter 3: Hiding in Screens..............................16
Chapter 4: Loneliness Unmasked.....................20
Chapter 5: Work Without Walls........................ 24
Chapter 6: Conspiracies in the Dark............... 29
Chapter 7: Faith and Fracture........................... 34
Chapter 8: Friends, Politics, and the Breaking Point...38
Chapter 9: The Body in Isolation..................... 42
Chapter 10: Parenting in the Collapse............46
Chapter 11: The Money Mirage........................ 50
Chapter 12: The Shadow That Remains........55
What Remains.. 58

What Was

We did not know how fragile normal was.
We gathered without fear.
We shook hands without pause.
We packed into stadiums, classrooms, airports, and churches without thinking twice about breathing the same air.

We complained about traffic.
We rushed through grocery lines.
We sent kids to school, expecting them to come home with nothing more than homework.
We sent kids on playdates without worry, never thinking twice about who they sat next to or what they touched.

Birthdays meant crowded rooms.
We blew out candles and ate the same cake.
The smell of popcorn in theaters.
The roar of stadium crowds.
Weddings meant full dance floors.
Funerals meant arms around shoulders instead of faces behind screens.

We traveled without hesitation.
Flights were inconveniences, not dangers.
Passports meant adventure, not risk.

We built routines without questioning them:
Nine-to-fives.

Sunday services.
Friday nights at bars.
Saturday morning games.

Everything felt guaranteed, repeatable, endless.
We lived with the illusion that tomorrow would look like today.
That the world would keep moving no matter what.
That nothing could stop it.

Until it did.
And when it did, the world looked different.

Author's Note

The pandemic didn't just stop the world. It stripped us bare.
Birthdays on Zoom. Fights in kitchens that doubled as offices. Sunday sermons playing on a laptop instead of a pew.

COVID didn't change us. It exposed us.
Behind closed doors, marriages cracked. Screens became survival. Loneliness got loud.
Some people became more themselves. Others disappeared.

I lived through the same blur you did.
Days bleeding into nights. Hope flipping into despair.
News alerts. Empty shelves. The quiet fear nobody wanted to name.
That silence told me more about people than any headline ever could.

It showed me what we cling to when nothing feels certain, and what we let go of when we can't fake it anymore.

This isn't a history book. It's a mirror.
And I'm holding it up to all of us.

Everybody hides.
The pandemic proved it.

— Brian B. Turner

Chapter 1: Behind Closed Doors

Couples

Before 2020, many couples did not question the health of their relationship. Work, commutes, errands, kids' schedules, and endless activity kept everyone moving fast enough to stay distracted.

Then the world stopped. What was left was silence, four walls, and two people sharing the same space every day.

Some couples discovered they had nothing in common once the noise disappeared. Arguments about who left dishes in the sink escalated into shouting matches about money, fidelity, or the future. Even the Wi-Fi became a battleground as Zoom meetings overlapped and bandwidth stretched thin.

The numbers told the story. By the end of 2020, divorce filings in the United States had risen 34 percent. Lawyers reported record caseloads. Domestic violence hotlines lit up with desperate calls. At the same time, surveys showed a rise in reported loneliness, even among people living with partners.

The pandemic did not create weak relationships. It revealed them. If a relationship was built on distraction, performance, or habit, lockdown stripped it bare. If it was built on trust, patience, and genuine connection, lockdown confirmed it.

Everybody hides. Couples hide behind busy schedules and planned escapes. But the pandemic stopped the hiding.

Families and Kids

The home became everything. School. Office. Playground. Church.

Parents found themselves staring at glowing screens, pretending to supervise virtual classrooms. In reality, many kids muted their teachers and spent hours watching YouTube or gaming while parents in the next room scrambled through their own work calls. For the first time, parents saw just how fragile the system really was.

Some families rediscovered each other. Meals came back. Siblings played together because there was nobody else. In households with patience and rhythm, the chaos pulled people closer.

But in fragile homes, the opposite happened. Constant proximity magnified every fracture. Quarantine forced every unspoken tension into the open. The American Academy of Pediatrics reported steep rises in anxiety and depression among children during lockdown. Screen time surged to record highs.

The pandemic did not create new family dynamics. It revealed the ones that were already there. The patient bent but did not break. The fragile snapped.

Friendships and Roommates

Friendships took a hit, too. Without bars, gyms, or office chatter to keep them alive, many friend groups went silent. Group chats faded. Promises to "catch up soon" turned into nothing at all.

Friends who once gathered weekly found out who could stand the silence. The pandemic turned masks into symbols and risk into excuses. It gave people permission to judge, to distance, to let go.

Others proved their depth. They found ways to stay connected, even in awkward drive-by birthdays, late-night FaceTimes, or care packages in the mail.

Roommates discovered truths they could not ignore. Some fell into an almost family-like rhythm, cooking together and sharing survival strategies. Others realized they had only been tolerable when life was easy. In apartments where one person hoarded supplies while the other panicked about rent, the tension never went away.

The silence stretched beyond apartments and houses. A Harvard study in 2021 found that 36 percent of Americans reported "serious loneliness" during the pandemic. Among young adults, it was 61 percent.

It was not just distance that ended friendships. It was the realization that many relationships had been running on autopilot all along.

Everybody hides. Friends hide behind group chats. Roommates hide behind shared rent and weekend outings. When those distractions vanished, so did the illusion.

The Echo in 2025

The doors reopened, but something broke that never came back. Divorce filings climbed. Friend circles shrank. Surveys say Americans have fewer close friends than at any point in modern history.

This is the legacy of lockdowns: people never relearned how to show up. Relationships became optional. Loneliness became normal.

The pandemic did not just crack intimacy. It rewired connection itself. And that is why so many are still alone, even in crowded rooms.

The real virus was not distance. It was disconnection. And five years later, we are still infected.

And that truth still carries forward.

The Thread

The pandemic did not create new realities. It stripped away the lies we hid behind.

Behind closed doors, people were not just stuck inside.
They were face-to-face with themselves.

And the verdict was simple. The virus did not break us. It unmasked us.

Chapter 2: The Masks We Wore

Balcony Life

In the first weeks of lockdown, balconies and windows became stages. People clapped for healthcare workers at 7 p.m. Neighbors played music across courtyards. Parties spilled into the night, with speakers blasting through concrete walls.

It looked like resilience. Sometimes it was. But often it was performance, a way of saying "we're okay" when the truth was something else.

One neighbor sang every night for three weeks, then stopped. The silence was louder than the music. The mask of cheer slipped. Exhaustion showed.

Public Masks

Masks were supposed to be about safety. They became symbols. To walk into a grocery store or board a plane, you covered your face. But the mask revealed more than it hid.

By late 2020, surveys showed that three out of four Americans believed mask-wearing was more about politics than public health. A strip of fabric turned into a declaration: of loyalty, of fear, of defiance.

The cloth mask was never only about protection. It was another way of hiding, hiding what side you were on, hiding your fear, hiding the fact that nobody felt certain.

Emotional Masks

Online, the feeds filled with curated versions of pandemic life. Bread baking. Whipped coffee. Home workouts.

But offline, depression spiked. Anxiety hit record highs. Alcohol sales jumped 54 percent in March 2020 alone. Friends called them "quarantine cocktails," but for many, they turned into a nightly blackout.

Social media made it worse. Studies showed that more time online during lockdown meant higher stress and depression. The happiest posts often hid the hardest nights.

Everybody hides. Some behind filters. Some behind routines. Some behind the smile that masks a breakdown.

The Echo in 2025

The masks came off, but the performances did not. People still curate who they are, hiding flaws behind filters and facades.

Workplaces reopened, but employees learned how to look busy without doing much at all. Friendships resumed, but many stayed surface-level, maintained through screens and highlight reels.

The pandemic did not invent pretending. It proved how natural it had become.

Five years later, we still smile for cameras, not for each other.

And that's the truth we carried forward.

The Thread

The pandemic showed us that hiding did not stop when the world shut down. It only shifted.

Some hid behind balcony sing-alongs. Some hid behind political symbols. Some hid behind curated feeds and cocktails blurring into the next day.

Masks came off eventually. The hiding never did.

Chapter 3: Hiding in Screens

Digital Playgrounds

When playgrounds and parks were closed, kids built new worlds on screens. Roblox playdates replaced recess. Discord chats replaced sleepovers.

On the surface, it looked harmless. Creative, even. But many parents realized their children were not just playing games. They were disappearing into them. Daily active users on Roblox doubled to more than 50 million by 2021. Hours that would have been spent outside became endless time building avatars and buying digital gear.

Screens became the safest place to hide.

Adults Online

Adults were not different. TikTok became the global escape hatch. Downloads broke records. People who swore they would never post found themselves lip-syncing, dancing, or ranting into their phones.

It felt like entertainment. But it was also avoidance. Behind every viral dance was someone trying to kill time, numb anxiety, or seek notice. Studies showed a direct link: higher social media use during the pandemic correlated with higher depression and stress.

The screen did not just distract. It swallowed hours, whole days, whole months.

Work Without Walls

Screens were not just for play. They became the office. Bedrooms turned into cubicles. Dining tables turned into boardrooms. Every meeting became another square on the grid.

Parents swore their kids were "in class" while the school tab sat open, with Minecraft running in the background. Workers stretched twelve-hour days into fifteen, pretending to be productive, while burnout quietly consumed them. One employee shut her laptop at midnight and cried in the dark, realizing the workday had no end.

Remote work jumped from 6 percent of the U.S. workforce to over 35 percent overnight. But productivity stats hid the real story, a workforce cracking behind the glow of a screen.

Screens blurred the line between who we were at home and who we performed at work.

The Darker Screen

Not all hiding online was harmless. When strip clubs and bars shut down, OnlyFans exploded. The platform jumped from 7 million users in 2019 to more than 85 million in 2021.

For some, it was survival. A teacher who lost her job turned on her camera to cover rent. For others, it was escape. Subscribers who swore they would never pay for intimacy spent thousands trying to buy connection.

Pornhub traffic hit record highs. Alcohol-fueled late nights blurred into scrolling sessions that never ended. For many, the screen became the dealer, the bartender, and the bedroom, all in one.

The pandemic did not just digitize our work and play. It digitized our secrets.

The Echo in 2025

The screens never turned off. Work moved back to offices, but meetings stayed on Teams. Kids returned to classrooms, but homework still lived on tablets. Entertainment never left the scroll. TikTok and YouTube became the new background noise of daily life.

Porn use stayed higher than before. OnlyFans grew into a billion-dollar industry. The distractions people leaned on in lockdown became habits they never let go.

The pandemic did not just trap us in screens. It rewired our attention.

Five years later, we no longer escape into screens. We live inside them.

And that is the world we carried forward.

The Thread

The pandemic proved that hiding did not require walls. It only required Wi-Fi.

Children hid in avatars. Adults hid in feeds. Workers hid behind digital grids. And millions hid in darker corners of the internet, where desire, loneliness, and survival met.

Screens did not just keep us connected. They kept us covered.

Chapter 4: Loneliness Unmasked

Silent Celebrations

Birthdays turned into drive-by parades. Relatives waved from car windows, tossing balloons and honking horns. Graduations were streamed on laptops, with names called to empty auditoriums. Funerals happened on Zoom, where grief was reduced to squares on screens.

No one forgets watching a casket lowered on a livestream while the sound cut in and out. Mourners muted, tears swallowed in silence. The ache of knowing you were not really there, that presence had been replaced by pixels.

Weddings turned into livestreams. A friend sent a link where once there would have been an invitation. On paper it was about safety, but everyone whispered what they already knew. He was cheap, and the pandemic gave him cover. Still, the excuse held. Most of us would have come.

The Hidden Epidemic

Lockdowns were meant to stop the spread of a virus, but they uncovered another crisis. Loneliness.

In June 2020, the CDC reported that 40 percent of U.S. adults were struggling with mental health or substance use issues. For young adults, one in four said they had seriously considered suicide in the past month. Living alone made it worse, but crowded homes could feel empty too. Many felt unseen in their own rooms.

Hotlines were overwhelmed. Calls to mental health services surged. Prescriptions for antidepressants climbed. People were alone even when they were not physically alone.

Loneliness was not a side effect. It was a parallel epidemic.

Coping in the Quiet

Some tried to mask the silence with new habits: baking bread, daily runs, virtual happy hours. But for many, these distractions faded. The quiet always returned.

Alcohol sales spiked by 54 percent in March 2020. Streaming services reported record subscriptions. Some people leaned on screens. Others leaned on pills. Loneliness did not always look like tears. Sometimes it was scrolling at 3 a.m. or drinking until the room stopped spinning.

In nursing homes, residents pressed their hands to the glass as families waved from parking lots. Some never saw each other in person again. Elsewhere, a woman lit a birthday candle by herself, sang softly, then blew it out in silence.

Everybody hides. Some in activity. Some in consumption. Some in pretending that the quiet did not hurt.

The Echo in 2025

Lockdowns ended, but loneliness did not. Studies show Americans report higher levels of isolation today than before the pandemic. Gen Z, the "most connected" generation, is also the loneliest.

Zoom funerals are gone, but the grief remains. Weddings returned, but the guest lists stayed smaller. Drive-by birthdays faded, but so did the effort to gather.

On Saturday nights, millions scroll TikTok alone, laughing at strangers instead of sitting with friends. For many, the glow of a phone replaced the presence of a person.

The pandemic did not just isolate people. It normalized absence.

We learned how to live apart. We never unlearned it.

And that's the silence we carried forward.

The Thread

The pandemic stripped away the noise that made life feel connected. What remained was silence.

Behind birthdays, behind parades, behind screens behind distractions, millions of people faced the same reality.

Loneliness was not the pandemic's shadow. It was its twin.

Chapter 5: Work Without Walls

The Vanishing Commute

When offices closed, millions thought they were gaining freedom. No more traffic, no more trains, no more dress codes. The commute disappeared overnight.

But the time saved did not turn into rest. It turned into work. People logged on earlier and stayed on longer. The boundaries that once separated office life from home life dissolved into a blur.

The Screen Office

Bedrooms turned into cubicles. Dining tables became boardrooms. Every meeting became another square on the grid.

Employees wore button-downs on top and sweatpants below. They smiled into webcams while juggling kids in the background. For some, the illusion worked. For others, it broke them.

Remote work spread faster than any policy shift in modern history. Within weeks, millions were working from bedrooms and kitchen tables.

Productivity reports claimed the transition was smooth, but beneath the numbers, exhaustion deepened and boundaries collapsed.

Parents insisted their children were focused on lessons while phones buzzed under the desk. Workers stretched days late into the night, some collapsing into bed with their screens still glowing beside them.

Everybody hides. Workers hid behind green dots on Slack, behind 'camera on' smiles, and behind digital busy signals masking exhaustion.

The Essential Divide

Not everyone had the privilege of hiding at home. Millions of workers in grocery stores, warehouses, hospitals, and delivery vans carried the weight of keeping society alive. They were called "essential," but most were underpaid and over-exposed.

While some employees hid behind screens, others faced packed shifts and empty shelves, risking exposure for low wages and little protection. Amazon reported record profits while warehouse workers reported record injuries. Nurses held phones up to dying patients so families could say goodbye.

The divide was clear. For some, work without walls meant working at home. For others, it meant working without safety.

Money and Survival

The workplace was not the only thing stripped bare. Money was too.

Millions filed for unemployment in the spring of 2020. Stimulus checks arrived, but they were lifelines that ran out fast. Some people hid their financial struggles behind closed blinds and quiet excuses. Others turned to side hustles, gig apps, or selling whatever they could online.

Fraudsters found cracks, too. Billions in Paycheck Protection Program (PPP) loans went to sham businesses or corporations that did not need them, while small shops and self-employed workers were left waiting. Families lined up at food banks in numbers unseen since the Great Depression.

Work without walls revealed how fragile the system really was. For some, survival meant a webcam. For others, it meant standing in line for groceries.

The Great Resignation

By 2021, the cracks showed in the numbers. Millions quit their jobs in what was called the "Great Resignation." Workers rethought what they would tolerate. Some left for better pay, others for peace of mind.

And it was not quiet. Workers posted resignation letters on LinkedIn, filmed themselves quitting on TikTok, and told their stories in viral threads. One barista walked out mid-shift, leaving a handwritten note taped to the espresso machine: *"Do not call me. I quit."* The photo was shared thousands of times.

Quitting became its own form of expression. For some, it was freedom. For others, escape. They were not running toward opportunity, but away from exhaustion, trauma, and workplaces that had shown their true colors under pressure.

The Echo in 2025

The commute returned for some, but the office never did. Millions still work hybrid, dialing into meetings from kitchens and spare bedrooms. For others, the promise of "remote flexibility" blurred into a permanent 24/7 workday.

The Great Resignation faded from headlines, but the distrust remained. Employees expect less loyalty from companies, and companies expect more output from fewer people. Burnout did not vanish, it calcified. In one global survey, a third of employees reported symptoms of burnout, proof the exhaustion never left

In cities across the country, gleaming office towers still sit half-empty, monuments to a workplace that never came back. And at home, parents still log into late-night calls with the glow of their children's bedroom lights in the background.

The pandemic did not just change how we work. It changed how we see work.

Five years later, jobs are no longer measured in hours. They are measured in what they take from us.

And that truth carried forward.

The Thread

The pandemic did not just move work into our homes. It exposed what work had always been.

Some jobs were built on performance. Others, on exploitation. Some people discovered flexibility. Others discovered fragility.

The walls came down, and with them, the illusions.

Chapter 6: Conspiracies in the Dark

The Virus of Doubt

When information changed daily, doubt filled the gaps. One week masks worked, the next, they did not. One month surfaces carried the virus, the next, they did not. People did not just fear the pandemic. They feared not knowing what to believe.

Into that silence, conspiracies thrived.

QAnon Goes Mainstream

QAnon had been fringe before 2020. By the middle of the pandemic, it was mainstream. Facebook groups with hundreds of thousands of members spread stories of hidden cabals, secret rescues, and government plots.

The uncertainty of the pandemic made wild claims feel possible. Parents stuck at home wandered into forums. Friends forwarded links they did not check. The line between skepticism and belief blurred in real-time.

Everybody hides. Some hid behind masks of certainty, shouting online as if they knew the truth.

Others hid behind silence, unwilling to argue with family members who had slipped deep into the rabbit hole.

The Misinformation Machine

YouTube views on conspiracy content soared, while Twitter became a battlefield of half-truths and doctored videos. WhatsApp groups traded miracle cures and secret warnings.

A Pew survey in 2020 found that more than 25 percent of Americans believed the virus was intentionally created in a lab, despite no evidence at the time. Others claimed 5G towers spread Covid. The crazier the claim, the faster it traveled.

For many, misinformation was not about facts. It was about control. Believing a hidden story felt safer than admitting nobody was in charge.

Snake Oil and False Cures

Fear created a market. Into it poured every cure, treatment, and potion people could invent.

Some sold essential oils and vitamins as shields against infection. Others pushed ivermectin and hydroxychloroquine despite little evidence. At the darkest point, a president suggested disinfectant injections on live television, and poison control hotlines spiked with calls.

The grifters thrived. Online shops, Facebook ads, and whispered recommendations promised immunity in bottles, drops, and powders. Millions of dollars changed hands. For many, it was less about science than hope. Buying something felt better than admitting there was nothing to buy.

One woman in Arizona drank fish tank cleaner that contained chloroquine after hearing it could prevent infection. She never woke up. Her husband ended up in the ICU. Their story was not unique. Fear blurred judgment, and the line between cure and poison vanished.

The Real Cost

The conspiracies were not harmless. They tore families apart. Some refused vaccines and never returned to the hospital. Others cut off relatives who "would not wake up." Thanksgiving dinners ended in silence, or shouting matches over articles no one could prove.

The pandemic showed how fragile trust really was. Not just in governments, but in neighbors, families, and friends.

Not every whisper was nonsense, though. Some rumors that sounded absurd in 2020 later proved true. The pandemic made people more suspicious, sometimes reckless, sometimes righteous. That was its double edge.

The Echo in 2025

The hashtags faded, but suspicion never did.. Conspiracies that thrived in lockdown outlived the virus. Some were absurd, but others were warnings disguised as rumors.

QAnon shrank, but questions about corruption, abuse, and power grew louder. It was whispered for years that celebrities and executives were hiding darkness. The pandemic gave people time to look closer. Some stories collapsed under scrutiny. Others came true.

The pandemic did not just create conspiracy theories. It sharpened doubt, sometimes foolish, sometimes justified.

Five years later, we no longer doubt the stories. We doubt the storytellers.

The Thread

Conspiracies spread faster than the virus, promising certainty in a world of chaos.

People were not just hiding from COVID. They were hiding from doubt.

Chapter 7: Faith and Fracture

Empty Pews

For centuries, faith meant gathering. They sang hymns shoulder to shoulder. Sharing communion. Hugging after service. In 2020, all of that disappeared.

Church doors were locked. Easter Sunday was streamed on Facebook. Pastors preached to cameras in empty sanctuaries. Believers bowed their heads alone in their living rooms.

The absence was jarring. Faith had always been collective. Suddenly, it was solitary.

Faith Online

Some adapted. Virtual choirs stitched voices together through Google Meet. Congregations prayed in YouTube chat boxes. Weddings were streamed, funerals were muted, and Bible studies met in Facebook Live rooms.

But screens changed faith. Rituals felt less sacred when interrupted by lag or low Wi-Fi. A pastor's sermon sounded different when the dog barked in the background. The divine felt distant when filtered through pixels.

Everybody hides. Some hid in livestream worship, typing 'amen' while scrolling on another tab. Others hid in silence, avoiding services altogether and calling it caution.

Fractured Beliefs

Faith fractured not only in practice, but in principle.

Some pastors defied lockdown orders, holding packed services in defiance of health rules. Others insisted faith meant submission, that protecting the vulnerable was the higher calling. Congregations split along the same political and cultural lines as the country.

One family fought every Sunday morning. The father believed missing church was a sin. The mother refused to risk sitting in crowded pews. Their teenage son rolled his eyes at both, calling the livestream a joke. What used to be a quiet ritual of worship became a weekly battle of conscience, of fear, and of pride.

In 2020, Gallup reported that U.S. church membership fell below 50 percent for the first time. The pandemic accelerated a decline already in motion. For many, absence became detachment.

Once the habit of gathering was broken, it did not return.

Faith as Refuge

Still, for some, faith deepened. The silence gave them clarity. The absence of crowds made prayer more intimate. People who had drifted came back to scripture. In crisis, some found not fracture but renewal.

In hospitals, nurses whispered scripture to patients dying alone. They held hands through latex gloves so the last words were prayers.

In homes, families knelt around kitchen tables, parents leading worship with cracked voices, children bowing their heads. For some, it was the first time faith had ever felt personal.

Spirituality became less about buildings and more about survival.

The Echo in 2025

The pews never filled back up. Attendance dipped during lockdowns and never returned to pre-pandemic levels. Many churches closed for good. Others survived online, but the screen could never replace the sanctuary.

For some, faith deepened. Families kept praying at kitchen tables long after churches reopened. But for many, the habit broke. Sundays became ordinary. The discipline dissolved.

The pandemic did not just fracture faith. It exposed who believed out of ritual and who believed out of need.

Five years later, faith did not vanish. It just stopped needing a building.

That truth never left us.

The Thread

The pandemic tested faith not by destroying it, but by dividing it.

Some discovered a new devotion. Others realized they had only been attending, not believing.

The pews were empty, and for many, they still are.

Chapter 8: Friends, Politics, and the Breaking Point

The Fractured Table

Politics had always divided families, but the pandemic made it a battlefield.
One side believed masks were safe. The other believed they were submission. One side trusted the vaccine. The other called it poison.

Thanksgiving dinners ended in shouting. Some ended in silence. A single headline or Facebook post was enough to split a table in two.
One family stopped speaking altogether after the father refused to wear a mask at dinner. He said it was his right. His daughter said it was her life.

Friendship on the Line

Group chats went dark. Friends unfollowed each other after one too many posts about lockdowns, protests, and the election.

A Pew study in 2020 found that nearly half of Americans had stopped talking to someone over political differences. The pandemic only added fuel to the fire. Beliefs about masks, mandates, and vaccines became identity markers, and friendships became collateral damage.

One twenty-year friendship ended with a single Facebook comment: *"If you believe that garbage, we're done."* Neither reached out again.

Everybody hides. Some hid behind memes, posting jokes laced with real venom. Others hid behind silence, avoiding conversations so they would not have to choose a side.

Protests in the Streets

While people stayed home, streets still filled. In the summer of 2020, protests after George Floyd's murder drew millions, masked and unmasked, chanting shoulder to shoulder. For some, it was the first time they had left the house in months.

At the same time, rallies against lockdowns erupted, with crowds waving flags, demanding the country reopen. Two different movements, two different truths, but both born from the same pressure: people who felt trapped, unheard, and desperate to be seen.

One young protester clashed with his own family. He marched for justice by day, then came home to parents who told him the protests were riots. At dinner, his silence said more than words.

The Political Pandemic

COVID became more than a virus. It became a political marker.
Surveys showed partisan gaps in everything from mask-wearing to vaccine uptake. News outlets painted two different Americas. For one half of the country, safety was a responsibility. For the other, it was control.

Trust collapsed. Not just in government, but in neighbors, coworkers, and friends. By 2021, it was possible to know someone's politics simply by whether they stood six feet apart.

The Echo in 2025

The shouting quieted, but the fractures never healed. Thanksgiving tables are smaller now, not from restrictions, but because invitations stopped being sent.

Some friendships ended during the pandemic and never restarted. A single Facebook comment turned into years of silence. Families split over masks and the wounds hardened into distance.

The pandemic did not just divide politics. It divided people.

The election ended. The division never did.

That fracture became the inheritance.

The Thread

The pandemic did not just test friendships. It tested loyalty, trust, and even truth itself.

Some ties bent and survived. Others broke and never returned.

The virus was not the only thing that spread. So did division.

Chapter 9: The Body in Isolation

The Quarantine Fifteen

When the world shut down, kitchens became cafeterias and couches became desks. People joked about the "quarantine fifteen," but it was not always a joke. Stress eating, late-night snacking, and endless delivery orders left its marks.

Some baked bread every weekend. Others stocked up on chips, frozen pizza, and comfort food. The pounds added up quietly, a reminder that the body keeps score, even when no one is watching.

One woman cried after trying on jeans she had worn easily the year before. It was not just about weight. It was about change she could not control.

Gyms Gone Dark

Gyms closed. Yoga studios locked their doors. For a time, even playgrounds were taped off with caution signs. People tried to improvise. Joggers ran in masks, gasping through cloth. Living rooms turned into makeshift gyms, with water bottles for weights and YouTube as the trainer.

But not everyone adapted. Equipment sold out, and motivation collapsed. A CDC study found that nearly half of U.S. adults gained weight during the first year of the pandemic.

Everybody hides. Some hid in sweatshirts, pretending the weight was temporary. Others hid in Instagram posts of home workouts they barely did.

The Rise of Fitness Tech

For some, isolation sparked reinvention. Peloton subscriptions soared. Fitness apps broke records. Trainers went live on Instagram, leading classes for thousands of people at once.

It looked like resilience, and sometimes it was. But it was also another mask. People posted workout screenshots and progress selfies as proof of discipline, even while struggling to keep it up off-screen.

Health Anxiety

The body was not only about weight. It was about fear. A cough became a warning sign. A headache meant panic. People sanitized groceries, scrubbed doorknobs, and flinched when strangers sneezed.

One man wiped down every grocery item with bleach wipes at midnight, long after his family had gone to bed. The ritual did not make him feel safe. It only reminded him how vulnerable he felt.

Google searches for "loss of taste" and "loss of smell" skyrocketed. Telehealth calls multiplied rapidly. Even minor symptoms carried dread. For some, every ache became suspicion.

The Echo in 2025

The gyms reopened, but the weight did not come off. Millions still carry the "quarantine fifteen," a reminder written into their bodies from a year when stress ate more than discipline.

Fitness apps and Peloton bikes kept booming, but so did the fatigue. For every success story of reinvention, there are quiet truths of people who never found their rhythm again. Burnout showed up in waistlines, in posture, and in blood pressure.

The fear lingered too. Some still flinch when someone coughs in a crowded room. Others keep the old habits alive, wiping grocery carts, sanitizing hands between errands, ordering groceries instead of entering stores. The rituals of panic hardened into routines.

Even the gym feels different. It used to be a place where people met, traded tips, or spotted each other. Now it feels awkward to approach anyone. Half the room is live-streaming workouts for followers, and the other half wonders if the person on the squat rack is performing for more than fitness. What was once community now feels like surveillance, and sometimes comedy.

The pandemic did not just change bodies. It exposed how bodies remember what minds try to forget.

Five years later, we no longer live in lockdown. But our bodies still do.

The Thread

The body never learned how to hide. It carried the weight, the fear, and the fatigue into every room we enter.

Everybody hides. At the gym, they hide behind cameras. At home, they hide in baggy sweatshirts. Online, they hide behind curated selfies.

The pandemic revealed the truth in flesh and blood: the body keeps score, even when we wish it didn't.

Chapter 10: Parenting in the Collapse

Classrooms Closed

Schools shut their doors. Classrooms turned into kitchen counters. Parents became teachers overnight, juggling math worksheets alongside work calls.

Laptops froze. Wi-Fi dropped. Teachers stared at rows of black squares. For kids, "school" meant logging in, muting, and zoning out. Parents pretended it was working, but most knew their kids were falling behind.

One little boy, missing his classmates, lined up stuffed animals on the couch and raised his hand to answer questions only he could hear.

The Weight on Parents

The burden fell hardest on families. Mothers left the workforce in record numbers, unable to balance jobs and childcare. Some parents quit altogether, while others worked until midnight trying to make up hours lost to online supervision.

A Pew study found that nearly half of parents with young children said they were "stretched beyond their limits." Some snapped. Others numbed themselves. less about enrichment than endurance.

Everybody hides. Some hid exhaustion behind smiling photos of "family game night." Others hid behind work, closing the office door while chaos raged in the next room.

One single mother admitted she cried most nights in the bathroom after putting her kids to bed. The kids thought she was fine. She was not.

Children in the Shadows

The collapse showed in the kids as well. Teenagers lost their proms, their sports, their graduations. Younger children lost routines, friends, and playgrounds.

One high school senior stared at a laptop screen during his virtual graduation while his parents clapped in the kitchen. A little girl asked her mom why she could not hug her best friend. A ten-year-old cried after missing an entire season of soccer.

The CDC reported that ER visits for children's mental health emergencies rose sharply in 2020. Behind muted microphones, kids were struggling.

College at Home

College students came back to childhood bedrooms, stripped of independence. Dorm rooms emptied. Campuses went quiet.

Some people tried to recreate a sense of freedom on Zoom happy hours. Others spiraled in isolation. Parents watched adult children regress, stuck between adolescence and adulthood and unable to move forward.

The image of a cap and gown in a living room became one of the pandemic's most haunting symbols of lost milestones.

The Echo in 2025

Schools reopened, but learning gaps never closed. Test scores for math and reading still lag below pre-pandemic levels, especially for younger kids. Teachers talk about "lost years," and parents know some of that loss is permanent.

Families adjusted, but not always upward. Many mothers who left the workforce never returned. Some parents rebuilt their careers. Others never recovered the momentum.

The rituals lingered too. Bedtimes drifted later. Screens became babysitters that never got fired. For kids, the line between classroom and entertainment blurred so much that even today, homework often loses to YouTube.

Even the family table changed. Pandemic "family game nights" didn't survive, but the habit of handing a child an iPad at dinner did. Parents laugh about it now, but beneath the jokes lies fatigue. For many, parenting has stayed stuck in survival mode.

The pandemic did not just collapse school schedules. It rewired family life.

Five years later, the collapse ended on paper. But at home, it never did.

The Thread

The collapse was never just about closed schools or canceled seasons. It was about the weight families carried in silence.

Everybody hides. Parents hide exhaustion behind smiles. Children hide struggles behind screens. Families hide their fractures behind routines that appear normal on the outside.

The pandemic revealed what parenting truly was: survival. And survival does not end when the news cycle moves on.

Chapter 11: The Money Mirage

The Panic and the Boom

In March 2020, millions believed the economy was collapsing. Stocks tanked. Jobs vanished. Headlines screamed, 'the worst downturn since the Great Depression." People lined up at food banks for the first time in their lives.

But behind the panic, money moved differently. By the end of the year, the S&P 500 was up 16 percent. Tech stocks hit record highs. U.S. billionaires added more than a trillion dollars to their wealth while millions clipped coupons and cashed stimulus checks.

One man panicked and sold his 401(k) when the market dropped, locking in losses he would never recover. His neighbor bought Tesla stock on a whim and doubled his money. The same street held two different realities.

The world looked like it was ending. For some, it was the beginning.

Crypto Gold Rush

Locked inside, people turned to digital bets. Bitcoin traded under $5,000 in early 2020. By the end of 2021, it was above $60,000. Overnight, early adopters became millionaires.

Forums filled with pandemic hobbyists-turned-day traders. Some gambled stimulus checks on crypto and bragged about doubling their money. Others lost everything chasing hype coins that collapsed as quickly as they rose.

It was not just an investment. It was an escape. While the real world stood still, the digital world promised movement.

Real Estate Fever

While renters struggled to pay landlords, homebuyers flooded the market. Interest rates dropped, demand exploded, and bidding wars broke out. Prices soared and so did inequality.

A young couple making offers on starter homes found themselves outbid again and again by investors with cash. Meanwhile, their landlord raised rent, citing "market demand." The American dream did not disappear. It was bought up by someone else.

The housing market told the story clearly: the pandemic did not freeze the economy. It fractured it.

Winners and Losers

From the outside, it looked like collapse. On the inside, money was consolidating.

Amazon's revenue jumped nearly 40 percent in 2020. Walmart and Target thrived while small shops closed forever. Zoom became a household name. Its stock soared 400 percent in a single year.

Meanwhile, restaurants shuttered. Salons disappeared. Family-owned businesses that survived generations fell in months. One shopkeeper stood inside her darkened boutique, boxing up inventory to sell on Instagram Live while the Target parking lot down the street stayed full.

The balance sheet of the pandemic was brutal: giants got bigger, and the small disappeared.

Everybody hides. Some hid in panic. Others hid in prosperity.

The Mirage

The pandemic economy was not what it seemed. Headlines screamed crisis, but markets boomed. People mourned jobs, but investors celebrated gains. One world feared collapse. Another quietly counted profits.

The mirage was simple: we thought we were all in the same storm. We were not even in the same ocean.

The Echo in 2025

The panic faded, but the divide widened. The stock market recovered years ago, but most households never did. Prices stayed high, wages lagged, and debt ballooned.

Crypto crashed, but not before it made millionaires who cashed out in time. Real estate cooled, but the homes bought at inflated prices stayed out of reach. The pandemic gains of the wealthy became permanent. The losses of the vulnerable did too.

Small businesses never came back in the same numbers. Empty storefronts still dot main streets, while Amazon vans fill those gaps. What felt like a temporary imbalance turned into a permanent reshaping of who gets to win.

The pandemic did not just disrupt the economy. It revealed the economy was never built for everyone.

Five years later, the mirage is gone. The divide is not.

The Thread

The pandemic showed that money does not disappear. It moves.

Everybody hides. Some hid in panic, pulling savings out of fear. Others hid in prosperity, riding the waves of crypto, stocks, and real estate.

The truth was always there. Crisis does not change who gets rich. It only reveals it faster.

Chapter 12: The Shadow That Remains

The People Factor

The virus was never the whole story. People were.

2020 showed us who they really were. Friends vanished when you needed them most. Families split into strangers over beliefs that should not have defined them. Neighbors drew lines where there used to be none.

The pandemic gave everyone an excuse to discriminate, to disappear, to distance. Some used health as the reason. Others used politics. But behind every mask and every argument was a choice: who mattered, and who never really did.

The Dark Cloud

It's 2025, and the cloud has never lifted. The world opened, but something stayed heavy in the air.

People still trust less, forgive less, invite less. Workplaces are fractured, families are smaller, communities are thinner. There is a silence now, not because of lockdowns, but because of distance that became permanent.

The grill on the back porch still rusts from a barbecue that never returned. Half the neighborhood stopped showing up, and nobody bothered to call them back.

The world changed in 2020. And we are still living inside that change.

The Echo in 2025

Five years later, it is not just about a virus. It is about exposure.

We learned who was selfish, who was shallow, who was loyal only when it was easy. We learned how quickly prejudice can be justified with fear, and how quickly friendship can collapse under pressure.

The pandemic didn't just test relationships. It revealed them.

Five years later, the world is open, but trust is not. And the dark cloud is still here.

The Thread

The pandemic stripped the world bare. It did not just reveal our health, our money, or our systems. It revealed us.

Everybody hides. Behind friendship, behind faith, behind loyalty, behind masks of love that turned out to be costumes.

The truth is simple. The pandemic did not break the world. It unmasked it.

And what it revealed is the shadow we still live under.

What Remains

The world says the pandemic ended, but you and I know better.

We still carry the silence in our friendships.
We still carry the fractures in our families.
We still carry the prejudice people justified with fear.

2020 showed us who people really were.
That friendship for some was only convenience.
That loyalty was real only until it cost something.
That kindness could vanish as fast as toilet paper from an empty shelf.

The kids never fully got their years back.
Classrooms reopened, but learning gaps remained.
Screens replaced teachers, YouTube replaced homework.
Childhood shortened. Parenting grew heavier.

The money never balanced either.
Stimulus checks came, and they went.
PPP loans saved some businesses, sank others.
Small businesses closed, and main streets emptied.
But Target thrived. Amazon thrived.
Crypto minted millionaires while families counted debt.

The game was never fair. The pandemic only made it obvious.

Travel collapsed too.
Passports sat in drawers.
Suitcases gathered dust.
The world shrank to living rooms and backyards.
And even after borders reopened, many never stretched their lives wide again.
We learned to watch the world instead of walk it.
Scrolling feeds replaced tickets.
Sunsets came through glass screens instead of plane windows.

Faith fractured too.
Pews emptied. Congregations split.
Some prayed at kitchen tables.
Others stopped praying at all.
We saw who believed from ritual, and who believed from need.
Work broke apart and never returned.
The cubicle died, but burnout lived on.
The corner office turned into the kitchen table.
Jobs stopped being measured in hours.
They were measured in what they took from us.

Loneliness never lifted.
The Zoom funerals ended, but the grief never did.
The balcony singalongs stopped, but the silence remained.
We learned how to live apart, and we never unlearned it.

The virus left scars.
But the people left shadows.

The doors reopened. The headlines moved on.
But the shadow never lifted.

That is the truth no one wants to say out loud.

The virus ended.
The hiding did not.

2020 never ended.

www.ingramcontent.com/pod-product-compliance
Lightning Source LLC
Chambersburg PA
CBHW020255090426
42735CB00010B/1929